MW00535285

POETRY BY EMILY JUNGMIN YOON

Ordinary Misfortunes

A Cruelty Special to Our Species

Find Me as the Creature I Am

EMILY JUNGMIN YOON

Find Me as the Creature I Am

/ Poems /

Alfred A. Knopf
NEW YORK   2024

THIS IS A BORZOI BOOK
PUBLISHED BY ALFRED A. KNOPF

Copyright © 2024 by Emily Jungmin Yoon

www.aaknopf.com

Knopf, Borzoi Books, and the colophon are registered
trademarks of Penguin Random House LLC.

Library of Congress Cataloging-in-Publication Data
Name: Yoon, Emily Jungmin, author.
Title: Find me as the creature I am / Emily Jungmin Yoon.
Description: First edition. | New York : Alfred A. Knopf, 2024.
Identifiers: LCCN 2023057595 | ISBN 9780593801185 (hardcover) |
ISBN 9780593801192 (ebook)
Subjects: LCGFT: Poetry.
Classification: LCC PS3625.O535 F56 2024 | DDC 811/.6—dc23/eng/20231218
LC record available at https://lccn.loc.gov/2023057595

Jacket illustration by Nadiuska and Priscila Furtado / Universo
Jacket design by Janet Hansen

MANUFACTURED IN CANADA
FIRST EDITION

For David

Contents

/ PROLOGUE /

What Carries Us

First, there was the horse.

Imagine creatures as majestic,
standing. All their lives they stand, withholding.

Imagine being tamed. Learning to be still,
to be speed. Imagine birds as large

as horses. We would be flying, grabbing
a majestic creature by its collar.

In cylinders of metal, we are four-legged
beast-lives of liminal spaces.

One time I was so tired of flying I wondered
if I would spend all my life packing then unpacking.

A complaint of privilege. We are such spending
creatures. And when I say we are beasts,

is that a metaphor? Metaphor, according to Papastergiadis,
is also transportation, between absence and presence,

"articulating action." Its "very process,"
in times of extremity, is "akin to prophecy."

I like the idea of transportation
as articulation, that the end of metaphor is a kind

of arrival, like getting off the train at an unknown stop.

So when I say we are beasts, perhaps what I mean
to do is remember that predators

have forward-facing eyes, and we do
grab others by the collar, and we do fly

in metal, in preparation for the kill.

What I want to do is slow down time.

Imagine love as a horse.

Think about us—a distance
apart only a flying thing could connect us—

standing and pacing, tamed and watching,

then finally with each other, laughing
as if to collapse, unbridled as wild horses.

In this era of brevity in this era of metal in this
era of abbreviation, yes, I'm trying to make you

think of me longer. Yes, this whole time,

the bird, the train, the whole thing
about metaphor, I said to say this,

that this is what carries us, the slow
consideration of what each other is.

First, there was the horse.

/ I /

All my friends who loved trees are dead

my grandmother said, and now she is.

/

In the first morning in a world without her, even as we all
tuck her into the earth, her children and their children,
stepping on the velvet soil, smooth and firm and new and old
all at once, I cannot accept the facts.

/

She had a green thumb. She loved medical shows.
How can you see all that blood, all that cutting? I asked.
She said, *I wanted to become a doctor.* She wanted
to travel the world. She taped the world
map on her table, drew a line from Chicago to Busan.

/

In the Field Museum, I stroll among *Birds of America,*
life-size paintings of specimen doing what they do:

a pair of long-billed curlews, standing next to tall grass.
A roseate spoonbill, twisting toward water.

Audubon went through great troubles, observing them flying
and looking after their young, then somehow,

killed these birds. Now here I am, observing
portraits, protected from the blood, the cutting.

/

Taking turns pouring dirt over her coffin,
her children comment how she chose the perfect day to go:

a warm Saturday with blue skies, too warm, in fact, for January.

She is so good at forecasting the weather, my uncle praises.

/

My mother studies the soil clinging to the living
left behind, my grandmother's trees.

I was able to keep the old yellow tree alive.

A face full of new light.

The Dracaena marginata had babies.
The angel's trumpets are blooming.

A mouth full of strange new names.

/

Walking through the Field, I see more animals
who loved trees, who died to pretend

in a taxidermy wing in Chicago. *I can't do it today,*
I text my friend, *I'll let her go some other time.*

Why do you have to let her go?

/

I loved the poetry she enclosed in her early morning
text. I loved the one that began: *I had trouble*
falling asleep. That she thought of me in that trouble,
in that trembling video she took of her kitchen.

/

In the Intensive Care Unit, I am annoyed.
At how beautiful the nurse is,

next to my grandmother's swollen hands and feet—
at the foundation, curly eyelashes, roseate blush.

Life, painted into display.

Then, I am ashamed.

/

Her grave is contracted for fifty years, another thing I learn—
where our bodies lie are temporary exhibits.

/

In her dawn poem, my grandmother wrote,

All my friends who loved trees are dead.

/

I received her sadness and named it a poem.

/

She loved me. She was tired of living.
I wanted to be protected from her death.

/

My mother enters the morgue, the only one
of the children to do so. She watches

her mother being cleaned and dressed.

She observes the blues and greens
of a dead body, its cold wings twisting out.

She curls out my grandmother's dried lips,

then, with her makeup, starts painting her.

I Close My Eyes to Paint Beauty

Nature in its efficient glamour:

the rose in its scalloped explosion,
the turtle's hexagons bounded by pentagons,
repeated in the wing of the dragonfly.

The pinecone. The broccoli. Sliced,
onto a plate that echoes the rose's design.

This patterning means nature is lazy, I once read—
artistry to expend the least for the greatest pain.

I mean greatest gain. I misspeak too often.

I admire nature's archaic methodology and cannot think it lazy.

How could I? Looking at the face
of the sunflower reiterating itself into a tremendous field.

A semblance of order, so they say, to chaos,
chaos being the violence of elements.

In the face of violence my face,
too, requires repetition. Stroke after stroke

of color, a dual purpose: cloak the evidence
and array the geometry of my anatomy.

My obsession for efficiency comes from somewhere.

Perfectly cat-eyed and glittered, I step out.

Love and Death Speaking at Once

We come together. To love someone means to imagine
their death. Two a.m. and you lie awake in fear of us. *What if?*

What if? Call your mother. Say you're sorry. Call your
father. What? Call your sister. Memory sustains

and fades. Take a picture. Keep a journal. Underline,
dog-ear, leave margin notes in your book, mark it

with your touch. Do not go into a mountain alone.
Write the letter that embarrasses you, adulating,

undulating language, each line a petal in a dahlia.
Fields of swaying dahlias, you make them.

Yes, you can. Give that person a bouquet of dahlias,
grown, then cut for you; that is us, together. We are beautiful

together. If we make in you such tenderhearted anticipation—
    is it so bad?

The Greenland Shark

It made sense: you have to keep living
beyond surprise for desire to return.

With antiquity returns beauty, she thought,
or rather, longevity is an attraction.

Growing long and old on her own, she had survived
centuries of names man had given to time,

such as what they called the Renaissance,
which was a good season

for their certain male specimen.
She thought she remembered a name

or two she was given by men
who saw her and left her alone,

because fear; because disgust.
Mercy—perhaps.

Through it all her heart renewed
its languorous beating so now

they want to know—What is your secret?
What is your soft body capable of?

Her fat liver could oil their killing machines.
Her flesh could drive a pack of sled dogs mad.

Cannibalism was not beneath her.
Wisdom? Please. She asked nothing,

and asked for none. No,
what she wanted was to eat in peace.

They want to know.
How she achieved her age,

how they could do the same.
This was the final desire her body held.

For some of them, anyway—
not these men whose livelihood depended

on the same fish she hunted,
who acted like they had permission to all life,

though they do own these decks—
on which she lay woven into their nets.

Listening still, listening to their anger.
That it wasn't her.

It was not even her that they wanted,
her heathered mass that carried her

through ancient ice and thaw,
and nobody asked her name.

Body Of

My mother, teaching me how to protect my body:
when a man touches you here, yell, *I am a body*
that will bear a child. How was I,
a child, to understand that as the sanctity
of my body. How was I to know to say,
The body without that potential is also whole
and holy. A man who touches a child
does not care whether she will one day be
fertile. A dear friend, on making the body
useful, encourages me to have
babies. What does it mean to say I have
my body. *I have a brain, you know, I have*
a life, a heart, I've said before, meaning
only mine, without knowing there were
outlines of other bodies fleshing in my center,
being the body of woman, for whom
body means collective. As it is for the body
of evidence. Of knowledge. Here I present my body
of work. My body of water. Here, my body,
body. But we, are we? Of our bodies? Bodies are thrown
across oceans, across lands. Bodies lie
bleeding through the evidence of bullets. Honest
bodies bleeding honestly. In order to continue living,
we try to leave evidence of our lives. We accumulate
bodies in whatever way we can. Men leave
themselves in women's bodies.
Friends, I am just now ready to love my own. I love
my father's eyebrows on my face and I love
my mother's calves on my legs and I love

the parts of my body that I do not name.
Let that be enough. The future of this land is uncertain
in how high the flames, the waters, will be.
This land in which I still bleed,
this land in which I give up
something every day.

Decency

When a man threw his fist into a wall next to my eye
I said that was love, that love was rage.
I was in the habit of loving anyone who laid a cold hand
on my face and said he'd pray for me.
Or anyone who prays. I thought apology
was love and so I loved to hear a man say sorry.
I loved to forgive because it meant I was a goddess. I forgave
because he couldn't possibly forgive himself.
There's a demon inside me, he said. Who cares if it's a demon
when it is mine and I am greedy for it. *No, and I don't care,*
do you hear me?—I'd say, and greed seemed to river
through my body. Even years later I could not speak of men
and their violence because I wanted to believe, yes,
in such a thing as decency in men I loved, that love
was decent. All the men who wanted me beautiful,
wanted me thin, wanted me with short hair, wanted me less
smart, wanted me, wanted me not, wanted me with pink
cheeks, wanted the best for me, wanted me in ruffled
skirts, wanted me naked, wanted me dead, all the men,
who wanted me, men who wanted, men who are
gone, not gone
enough.

Affection

We watch the moving topography of brutality, the red slopes
and orbs mapping deaths from virus, from fire, from firearms.

It feels impossible to think *red* and visualize beauty and yet
red roses are splashed all around the city, so brazenly alive

that they stupefy me. People stop, pose, take pictures
of their loved ones under the mess of flowers.

I love the red beak of the rose-ringed parakeet even after I find
the threat they pose on the land I live. *Affection* means both
 fondness and *disease.*

Words reflect the world, which is to say nothing makes sense.
If we say only civilization can *finish* the world,

does it mean *to complete* or *destroy?* If we say the world might
 weather—
to endure or *wear away?*

The Blades

You cut down on the gopher in a single, crisp stroke
in the garden. In it also, your mother's prized orange tree.
A blue jay your family feeds and has trained.

I picture the gopher, no longer struggling in the trap
inside the water pipe for the sprinkler
throbbing over grass and stones.
Then, you must have slid open the door
to the dining room, leaned the shovel on the tree.
I heard this story years ago in California.

In the time of pandemic, alone together, I read
too much news: "Trump Defends Using 'Chinese Virus' Label,"
"Woman Assaulted in Manhattan, Blamed for COVID-19,"
"Racism Is a Virus." I obsess, knowing

our place as Asians in this country,
the exemplar minority with advanced degrees and
gadgets, a superior meekness. Knowing,
our desirability was built to reassert Western centrality.
That, too, a type of technology.

To keep us in check, a Texas man took it on himself
and stabbed an Asian father and two sons,
cutting their faces open. One of the children has a gash
pointing to his eye, the damage itself in the shape
of a blade. A delta. Wanting to breach another opening.

Watch. Watch the wild turkeys roam the neighborhood,
unconcerned, banal, and ugly.

Yet you love these animals.
When our friend's old cat died, you had cried.
He was eighteen, had a good, adored life.
You had mourned so, for someone else's animal.
So when your mother told me at the dining table
about the gopher, I was shocked.

But that, too, was kindness, your shovel.
For the slowly dying animal, injured beyond saving
for entering the human world in the shape of a pipe.
A wet reach to a diorama of the natural world.

Embarrassed and ashamed, you looked away.
As we sat, in that moment, two Koreans
in a white world, I wanted to marry you.
To protect the person who loves like no other.

Foolish and naïve, yes. Every day someone leans the shovel
and knife, real and not, against a gentler thing,
after striking another that looks like us.
For crawling too close, out of the technology they built.

Yet today, feeling momentarily safe
in our room, I can ask what you did with the gopher.
You buried the animal, you say.
In the same earth it came from.

/ II /

I leave Asia and become Asian

I am new in Victoria, a beautiful city tucked in at the very corner of British Columbia, on Vancouver Island. It resembles London: quaint buildings, charming waterfront downtown, a range of mild oceanic temperatures. A paradise, a town for "newlyweds or the nearly-deads."

Less than a year has passed since 9/11. Too nice for racism to exist, my parents are told.

Canada, a safer country, they figure.

We are met with assumptions—wishes—that we are Chinese or Japanese. The question "What kind of Asian are you" is novel.

I absorb English.

I accept that I am now "Asian."

I am now simultaneously more than and less than Korean.

/

I settle into sixth grade at my new school. One of the few Asian girls in class tries to befriend me.

Call her N. She is loud, bright, and always cheerful.

Our classmates scrunch up their noses when N opens her lunchbox.

When N brushes against them, they yell, "Ew, cooties!" sometimes replacing "cooties" with "germs," to which I ask, "Hey, Fred, what are cooties?"

Walking home, white boys from our class throw eggs at N from across the street.

N's stoic eyes, and her slow gait. Shells falling around her.

This teaches me.

I need to scrub clean my alienness so they don't think I, also, have germs, smell disgusting.

I begin to keep a diary, which I make sure to record in English.

/

On March 16, nineteen years later, I pick up my phone and see a headline. A young white man has shot and killed eight people, across three massage shops in the Atlanta area.

The names of the dead are Xiaojie ("Emily") Tan, forty-nine; Daoyou Feng, forty-four; Hyun Jung Grant, fifty-one; Suncha Kim, sixty-nine; Soon Chung Park, seventy-four; Yong Ae Yue, sixty-three;

Delaina Ashley Yaun, thirty-three; Paul Andre Michels, fifty-four. The last two customers, the others employees.

The killer claims that he had a sex addiction and wanted to eliminate the temptation.

The women's bodies, repositories of his temptation.

The police spokesperson on the case says the killer was "pretty much fed up," "kind of at the end of his rope."

Says, "Yesterday was a really bad day for him."

/

Suncha. My grandmother, my mother's mother, is also named Sunja, a different transliteration but nevertheless the same name.

Thirteen and obsessed with death, I confess to my grandmother my preoccupation.

She reassures me, saying, "By the time I was sixteen, I wasn't scared of anything in the world."

Death has already touched her life too many times. I look forward to turning sixteen.

/

Kukmin Ilbo reports that Suncha Kim moved to the United States in 1980.

Forty years later, gun violence is unfathomable in South Korea.

Suncha has a son, a daughter, and three grandchildren. In her spare time, she likes to line dance.

/

At sixteen, there are times when I feel immortal.

/

At sixteen, my best friend, S, a Chinese Canadian girl, and I exchange commentary: "If you're Asian, you automatically get fifty more points in attractiveness."

We recognize that Asian fetishization exists. What we don't know: danger. The Western history of dehumanization attached to it.

When grown men whistle at us as we roam downtown in mini-skirts, we giggle and strut with pride.

/

Much later, I read about the history of the Asian American movement. I find that "Asian American" is a political term from the sixties, in a drive toward Pan-Asian solidarity against the larger culture of racial oppression.

What do we imagine when one utters the word "Asian" or "Asian American"? An East Asian face? Like mine? Do I see my face in that world? Whom are we addressing, referring to, including, excluding? In using the terms without rigor, introspection, are we reasserting a certain supremacy?

/

Toward the end of seventh grade, walking home with N, I say something about being Asian. About how everyone expects me to be quiet, good at math. (Which are, in fact, both true for me.)

"You know, I'm Asian too," N says.

"You are?"

"Iraq is part of Asia."

/

Now that I live in the U.S., and my parents in Korea, all they are curious about is my safety wherever I go.

Is there discrimination against Asians? they want to know.

To that, where do we begin?

Every time there is a shooting, my mother hints that maybe I should move back to Korea.

"But my life is here," I say.

/

Soon Chung Park's husband, Gwangho Lee, says that he called her up one day just to tell her he missed her. It made her so happy. He laments that he didn't do it more.

Now her life is no longer here.

/

I read Jean Chen Ho's essay "Sex Work Is Care Work," tender recollections about her Chinese American aesthetician and Korean hairstylist in L.A., weaved into reflections on the Atlanta shootings and sex work as care work.

"I want to love them," she writes, regarding the victims. "I want the families and friends who survive them to know these women were valuable. For all the care they gave, all the times they administered or yielded touch. I want to touch back."

I think about the body scrub I get every time I go back to Korea. I, too, have paid women to touch me in bathhouses. The bathhouse women converse among themselves as they scrub clean their clients, laughing between strokes. Naked and surrounded by naked women, safe amid all our denuded, desexualized beings.

/

Hyun Jung Grant keeps her Korean citizenship.

She has two sons, works late hours at Gold Spa to pay for rent and their tuition.

She is one of those moms who are their children's best friend. She, too, loves to dance.

Unable to legally prove their relationship, the sons cannot obtain her body after the shooting.

/

The Asian body as a vehicle of germs, disease, illness.

At least for East Asians, I know this is not a new trope that rose alongside COVID-19. It is one that has persisted throughout the histories of East Asian migration in the U.S.

But the model-minority myth is such a strong, pervasive one that many East Asians themselves don't realize until the virus that we were still deemed threats, perilous, nasty.

That the narrative can change just like that.

/

Asian American Community in Shock, Asian American Community Petrified, How to Support the Asian American Community.

Am I part of this community? Is nationality a prerequisite for membership? What is the difference between "people" and "community"?

"Community" requires building. If we claim membership to such a broad category, the "Asian American community," imagine it as fellowship, friendship, family, we must ask—what work does it entail?

What have we been given by others, and what can we give?

How do we touch back?

/

In 2007, one month shy of turning sixteen, I read about a mass shooting at a place called Virginia Tech. The next day, on a stairway at school, a boy stops me to say:

"Hey, he was Korean. Are you going to shoot everyone too?"

His laughter,

and that of the other Taiwanese international students standing with him,

falls around me.

/

Yong Ae Yue moves to the U.S. to be with her military husband. They separate in 1982.

Even when she herself doesn't have work, she extends kindness to others, giving them food, flowers, gifts.

/

"Asian" and "Asian American" feel at once too big and too limiting.

Without an American passport, what does it mean if I say I am part of the Asian American community?

For now, I decide, it means to align myself with the lineage and the history of resistance to Whiteness. With the allegiance to community building across Asian-descent peoples in the country I live in. It means to extend kindness to those whose experiences and backgrounds are unfamiliar to us. It means to "speak nearby," in the words of filmmaker Trinh T. Minh-ha, and which Cathy Park Hong describes as speaking "in proximity (whether the other is physically present or absent), which requires that you deliberately suspend meaning, preventing it from merely closing and hence leaving a gap in the formation process."

It means to acknowledge, thus dispel, the notion that East Asians have representative status in both "Asian" and "Asian American." It means to use critical language to continue complicating and challenging these categories as well as "community," terms we often automatically insert ourselves in, all the while leaving out others, without asking what these acts mean.

I *become myself* an Asian American.

/

When nothing makes sense, how can I write?

Then I remember that I came to write precisely because little made sense—my linguistic, ethnic, cultural, racial, and gender identities, reflected and refracted in ways I didn't always expect, want, or understand, in the countries I came to call home.

Ever since I bought my first journal to become my own historian, writing has been an act to preserve myself against forces that try to diminish and distort me.

In an interview in Korea, someone asks me, "When there are so many tragedies, issues, how can we possibly remember them all?"

We can remember more than we believe.

I write to render that into truth, to try.

/

Poet J and I read together one Chicago afternoon.

We talk about how excited we are for our books to take on new lives, pass through different hands beyond ours and our friends'. We talk about people already asking what's next, what's next, what's next. What now? What are you working on now?

"I'm working on my life, damn it," J and I joke, and laugh, shoulders touching, two people of color who would never have met if not for our love of verse, who one day threw our hands in the air from our respective seats on this earth, and said, *Let us have beauty,* the page thickening with lines, through skyscrapers, through half-lit rain, driving south, through abundant darkness that is, without fail, too early and firm in its descent, Lake Michigan quiet through our windows, which we know is there, making its cold sounds against stone.

We're working on our lives.

/ III /

Litany for the Green

When I was five, my grandfather took me to the tomb
    of King Suro, lifted me over the stone fences

      & watched me slide down the mound over
and over again. Did he do this because he was

        an old man, because he didn't know where young
            parents take their children, like the aquarium

        or the water park or the toy store? Or did he
because he was once a child who never went

        to any of those? Was it because I was a child,
who he assumed would enjoy sliding

        endlessly? And wasn't he right? About how children
            conceive time differently, or that their imagination

        works differently, and that every slide was, in fact,
            different? Or did he do this because he was

        an old man who thought the only destination left
        for him was the grave? Or did he not care about death

and ancient bodies? Had he become indifferent
    to sacred things, like a young mother

hung over a stone fence with a child still crying
    on her back, or his village burned

to the ground? Did war take his morning
and night, his conception of time?

Did he know my grandmother then,
    a young woman waking to amber light

    from his village, thinking it was morning?
Did he do this because the park keeper, also

an old man, let him? Was he an old man?
        Was my grandfather? Was he old

    at all? Was she ever an old woman, his mother,
    whose grave he died on, cutting its grass?

Elsewhere

A burro walks into a lake and kills herself
after losing her newborn, and I believe in an elsewhere.

When my dog died, the other dog
did not kill herself. She did not walk from room to room or stop
     eating.

Theorists have wondered, does animal suicide mean *suicide,*
meaning, do animals speculate about the future,

meaning, do they understand death. I think what they mean
is whether animals know that death means the *end,*

the whales beaching themselves, the dolphins
ceasing to breathe, the deer leaping off a precipice

leaving behind a pack of hunting dogs, my dog
who died, my dog who did not kill herself—

and I want to say when the donkey stepped
into the water and when the whale leaned

against the aired sand and the deer leapt
into the sky, they chose an elsewhere,

which is not to say the end.
My mind is often elsewhere. My dog knew

the other dog was elsewhere, wherever that was.
Elsewhere, the wild moon spins with its moons,

bottlenose dolphins sway in sleep. A tree grows fruit
in a dream. When Kathy the dolphin was captured

and put elsewhere, perhaps she thought the way to move
to another elsewhere was to change her breathing, her body.

Do you think I am an optimist and a romantic?
I am terrified of death and dark

and hell and heaven. But here, now, because of the burro, I believe
in elsewhere, I swear, that when I am dead I'll be there,

wherever that is, but truly,
I'll be everyone else's elsewhere, when everyone is everywhere

else, which is to say is also elsewhere.
I'll be elsewhere,

just as how here, now, I am, in my room, alone,
anonymous to every lake I've never touched.

We do not have to touch everything we love

My gratitude honors no one but me.

My friends are lonely. We all are

so we eat and watch the world

burned and swallowed by the rest

of us. When we watch each other,

we are watching ourselves.

I will take every distraction I can get!

Because, yes, I insist, I deserve it.

Protect me, protect me.

People like me more when I'm silly

but I've forgotten how to make jokes.

All I'm left with is seriousness.

I am busy with everything. Everyone is busy trying

to laugh. The seal and the turtle are trying

to sleep. The dolphins are trying

to sleep. No, there is no "eco-friendly" way to swim with dolphins.

We do not have to touch everything we love.

We hate those who outlive us.

Bless the rats. Bless them and the raccoons

for not knowing proper etiquette with property.

Raccoons crawl frothing at their mouths

out of attics in this heat wave.

Eaglets jump off their nests in this heat wave.

Bless the AC in this heat wave, we yell.

There is no water and too much water all the time.

Can I have another mimosa here?

Please. Someone. I am starving.

I haven't seen a dragonfly in years.

In all the futures

You are still on the island we love,

you are in a bathtub, twice framed by water,
and let's say in this scenario,

the red-whiskered bulbul that was born
outside our door by the desiccated toad
is now seventy years old.

Say we believed enough times
with thorough sincerity the promises

that we will happen to die
on the same day.

For all these years, we let the old waves
fold over our ordinary heads

never hurting us,
generous, full,

shining with ancient lives
softening in the kind of alone
no earthly darkness can know.

Every day, I labor to hope.

That the ocean stays unskinned

of its ice and you always have water
to spare. Now let's imagine that I went

happy, sure of this. And you
are healthy and nowhere close to dying.

Selfish, I know. I always have been.

In all the futures I am capable of prayer for,
you are not alone—you are alive.

In the age of goodbyes I

stroke the waves and their luster,
arms around glassy skin. Face

the dead contents of its body:
white coral fades and emerges

among the strands of sun
curling the water. Among the pale entrails

fish nevertheless peck and feed,
bright silver, charcoal, jade, lemon, cherry,

sweet, and still, and frantic.
I have needed, *needed* so many colors

myself, plastic, polyester pleasures, red
meats, leathered elegance.

Lines of fingers human and machine
peck at the seams to feed my pleasure

far away from me. I rejoice
in my silver dress, cutting my steak.

Pleasure is not the same as joy, I'm told.
But if pleasure is all one can afford?

Blame the corporations, not the individual, I'm told.
I understand. I understand it all, so cure me of this self-pity.

Corporation. It comes from *corpus:*
body, dead body, animal body.

Six thousand fathoms deep, dim faces quiver
in the Mariana Trench. Anna and Elsa,

printed on a balloon, smile brightly for the camera
probing the abyss. In *Frozen II,*

they set out to save their world
from colonialism, environmental crises.

No one is too small to make a difference,
not even a balloon.

What should I do? How will you
live through this time? I say, flailing my arms.

To the old body of the unanswering sea,
our age of goodbyes—goodbye to the smooth handfish,

the splendid poison frog, the poʻouli, the ivory-billed
woodpecker, the western black rhino, the ʻolulu,

our homes, our enchanted forests, ancient rivers,
our memories and our spirits, beloved, our beloveds—

is but a puncture, a rivulet
in time, it does not have a say,

it has nothing left to say to us,
whether we stay, whether we go.

Related Matters

I look at the ocean like it's goodbye.

Somewhere, it is touching a land laying prey to fire.

My grieving mother brings the forest inside, a green excess.

When she repots the trees, it is not unlike changing diapers.

But she no longer tends to the small abject frames of the dying.

These days, everything feels like the end.

A few days ago, a typhoon shaved glass off buildings.

A woman in her sixties bled to death after it cut

the window into her arm. The name of the wind, Maysak,

means *teak tree* in Khmer, I learn. *The timber*

retains its aromatic fragrance to a great age, I learn. I am always

learning. What is it that I want

to know? There is nowhere in this world

that I want to live. I look at your face

like it's goodbye. There is nowhere to go.

I shut my window because what else

can I do. Tomorrow's typhoon is called Hǎishén,

meaning *sea god* in Mandarin. I confess

I want to live. Nowhere, but still, with great desperation, I want.

What is it that you want?

Tell me, is your face the same as mine?

Tell me, do we see the same things?

Tell me we are the same eyes

burning through the night.

Gray Areas

I want nothing to change, then wait for my life to change.

/

I move through gravel and mud
and arrive at the falls.

Unfattened yet
by rain, the water twists
its thin body over heathered rock.

I do not have a say in this.

Neither tourist nor local on this land,
I wonder at the beauty of this land

and wonder what the beauty of this land
has to do with me.

/

It took me years to commit to page my own history
and so I wonder how to write into my poem that palm

shading my house, that mother cardinal feeding
her young, who appears bigger than her

with his trilling puffiness, whose brown head
will soon burn red, just like hers,

that Jackson's chameleon in the cloud forest
swaying as he walks, copying leaves in the wind,

his globular eye turning and turning,
that poison dart frog who has no poison

because of the diet here, that snail and
that toad sitting together in the rain,

discussing a secret—
without questioning their origins and place.

/

What do I have
to do

with this place?

/

It's true even love has tired me before.
A tire I must pull through mud, water, sand.

I do not want to be strong. I want to lie down.
In the water. In the mud. In the sand.

I appeal to the ocean to release me of this fatigue.
I am holding on too much, too many,

the ocean says, pushing me out onto sand,
onto land where I splay my burning body.

/

Into the ocean two million tires pour out.

Off the coast of Florida, with the blessing
of the U.S. Army, to create a marine habitat.

A gold tire is dropped from a blimp
to christen this new cradle.

The tires, breaking loose and pummeled
by hurricanes and tropical storms,
choke corals, tumble onto sand.

Grief already too heavy a carriage to cradle *reef.*

/

I want my life
to be a poem. I want my life to be
a poem. The future of a poem is mystery.
Writing toward uncertainty, I locate beauty.
In this process I harvest joy.

/

Heavy rain floods Korea.
Heavy rain floods Libya.
Heavy rain floods Pakistan.

Watching the thin body of the polar bear on the thin body of ice,
the camera says, *We can't interfere with nature.*

Let it starve.
Let it starve.
Let it starve.

/

In the gray flood the brown cow swims for the first time.

Atop the asphalt the escaped zebra runs for the first time.

The pearl stomach of the beached marlin touches sand for the first
   time.

It is too dangerous to release a marlin into an ocean filled with
   tourists.

Under "Harvest" on the NOAA Fisheries website, it says, *Blue
   marlin are a favorite*

*target for recreational fishermen, as the fish tend to put up an incredible
   fight when hooked.*

/

The kingdom in which I find myself feeds me
and loving it is at once easy and complicated.

Between wanting nothing and everything,

I lie in the sand. I stand from water.

In this process I harvest _____.

Mudflat Story

Follow the curves of the mountains, highways, the Saemangeum
   Seawall, the longest man-made dam, beyond the Kunsan
   Air Base, Eighth Fighter Wing, the *Wolf Pack* of the Seventh
   Air Force, which is a part of the Pacific Air Forces, which
   is headquartered in the Hickam Air Force Base in Hawai'i;
   follow the airport operated by the United States Forces
   Korea; follow the faded fishing villages; follow the migration
   of shorebirds, the spoon-billed sandpiper, great knot, Far
   Eastern curlew, grey plover, the water deer printing their
   hooves on the mud; follow the eyes of people who name the
   flat Sura, embroidered silk; follow the husks of the green
   mussel, razor shell, overbite clam, Trapezium clam, marsh
   clam, which, waiting for the high tide that cannot come,
   not anymore, leapt out with their dry frames at the touch of
   rain, into water that cannot save them—look. Look at it all,
   and now tell me your story, a story that has not ended and
   so must speak, *There is life here. There is life here.*

Gala

One evening the summer sun isn't enough.

We, poets from the South & West, in the U.S. sense of the words,
and the East, in the global sense, walked through a blade of
 Vermont,
in sunglasses, in lace-up boots, in zigzag, in jeans,
 commenting on

 a beauty so murderous and magical it emancipated
some of us hundreds of years ago, for us to hear, *You should feel
 lucky
to be in this country.* One of us looks out at the rows of yellow
 flowers
and says, *Can you imagine arriving at land like this, thinking, How
 beautiful—*

I'm going to take it? Which reminded me of another friend, this
 time in Paris,
looking around its gilded splendor to say, *Look what Empire is
 capable of.*

Which reminded me of another friend, this one from Paris,
 looking down
at Seoul from a gold observatory to say, *It's kind of ugly.* & it felt as
 if he had said I am.

One evening of summer in Vermont,
we are beauty in sunglasses and embroidery and flower crown and
 plaid, cocktails,
our languages in our hands. Delicious & loud. We are at a gala

for writers. *What does "gala" even mean,* one of us asks,
to which another one says, *I think it's a kind of party,* to which
the first one says, *No, motherfucker, I want the etymology.* & we flare
    in laughter.

Two years later I consult the Online Etymology Dictionary to see
    gala (n.)
1620s, "festive dress or attire" (obsolete), from French en gala,
perhaps from Old French gale "merriment," from galer "rejoice, make
    merry" (see gallant).

See, gallant, in our festive red dresses and snapbacks and public
    merriment
and skins, razing through this country on the hayride, some of us
    standing
through the turbulence of it all, touching the berried shrubbery
    and August dirt,
indulging in a gala. See here, party of us, siblings—
        what did we sing in our hot breath?

One evening, we looked up at the sky and I asked about the man-
    given names
of its elements: *Is it Andromeda? Is it Venus?*

None of us knew shit. We asked anyway.

One evening we saw small wings
glittering over the same yellow flowers,
& knowing they were butterflies in hundreds to repopulate the
    land, sat astounded.

We had only days ourselves to fly
back to the South & the Midwest & the West, in the U.S. sense of
    the words.
The summer sun went promptly. Fastidious with its red folds over
    the sky.

    We lit the candles anyway.
    We passed the bread. We passed the wine.

        If the only world is a hell with my siblings,
I thought, *I should feel lucky to call this world home.*

Brother,
Sister,

I am here.
I walk with you.

Evolution

I look for uncomplicated peace in ocean and sand,
afraid of the kind of candor you draw
from me, my cowardly deep-sea regime.

With easy honesty I make utterances ugly and necessary
to my being, a kind of nakedness I never attempted
in the privacy of myself.

Looking at your back darkened by the sun
faithfully pouring into the water in front of us,

I think *desire* is the wrong word
and *love* too plain, *devotion* too sacred.

My whole life, I think, I will use for describing you.

What do I know outside of words, which despite their history
and combinations, are too few and short for this life.

I don't know if I want heaven,
but I know I want to be

where you go—
in sand, water, every possible
animal form.

Vow

I love you; I don't know how else to begin.

How we began, though, was almost as if
it were already written. The details of how we arrived

at each other, to say *I love you* even as we fall asleep,

to let each other's name be the first sound
we utter every morning, can only be a gift of careful construction,

a design of an elsewhere where we were already together.

Saying nothing, you make me want to live
more meaningfully. The world is so wild, beautiful,

and terrifying, and everywhere we turn, a new atrocity.

Then, I close my eyes and picture joy.
Among things, there is this day. Among faces,

there is yours. And I am no longer afraid.

I watch you in your own, quiet moments,
and I want this life. I want this life

to be longer. All I want is more time with you.

I love you.
This is the only way I know how to end.

/ EPILOGUE /

Next Lives

We roam and turn over stones at night
for signs of life, for food. We have yet
to risk our lives for light of day. The sun is cold

in its mercilessness. Our eyes worship the moon
but the sky dresses often in haze.

We float on structures over what used to be
a scenic highway. I say *structure* because it cannot be called
a house. If we are lucky, we have books and albums

with photos of luxury our ancestors enjoyed.
Every year was proclaimed a point of no return

for the climate, but we do not believe it. We cannot
believe so many would let us suffer. Yet
there is no other explanation. There are no

water mansions. There is no country.
She must have saved the country in her past life

to meet him, people say, of the lucky coupling.
In this life, I have hurt people.
Every year, I resolve to be kinder, then fail.

I love you and I dread the future.
I dread the future and I can't wait

to keep living with you. *Promise me you will find me*
in our next life, I urge. I have no confidence
I won't be born non-human. Or maybe that

will be considered lucky. Maybe I am not lucky enough
to be born a beautiful bird.

Brushed by wind into the night, you lift a stone.
You find me as the creature that I am,
staring up at you.

Acknowledgments

These publications housed (earlier versions of) poems in this book:

Action, Spectacle: "Affection"
The Believer: "Love and Death Speaking at Once"
Chicago Reader: "The Greenland Shark"
The Cut: "I leave Asia and become Asian" (published as an essay,
    "I Became Asian When I Left Asia")
Los Angeles Review of Books: "The Blades"
New England Review: "Elsewhere"
The New Republic: "Evolution"
The New Yorker: "Related Matters"
The Paris Review: "Decency," "Litany for the Green"
Pleiades: parts of "All my friends who loved trees are now dead"
    (published as "Field")
Poetry: "What Carries Us"
The Rumpus: "Gala"
The Sewanee Review: "In all the futures"
Toybox: parts of "All my friends who loved trees are now dead"
    (first written and published in Korean as "Cheoeumeuro
    Saranghan Saram" [처음으로 사랑한 사람, One I Loved First])
Virginia Quarterly Review: "Body Of"

Deep thanks to all the editors of these issues who invited me to
submit and/or accepted my works, and the other staff members—
assistants, managing editors, web editors, and more—who helped
make the publications happen.

The line "No one is too small to make a difference" in "In the age of goodbyes I" borrows from the title of Greta Thunberg's 2019 book.

The lines "The timber / retains its aromatic fragrance to a great age" in "Related Matters" come from the online *Britannica* article on teak.

The indented lines in "Gala" are borrowed and adapted from works by these poets, in order of appearance: Michael Torres, Paul Tran, Sebastián Hasani Páramo, Michael Shewmaker (couplet), Dustin K. Pearson. Thank you, my friends. You never cease to inspire and warm my heart. We *will* start our "What the Fuck is This?: A Podcast" someday.

Because of my pod of writers, artists, translators, and scholars I've been lucky to call my mentors and friends, I don't ever feel like I am writing alone. A special shout-out to folks who read early work, recommended or invited me to life-changing opportunities, or sat through countless hours of me spilling my woes in the past few years: Michael Bourdaghs, Wo Chan, Cortney Lamar Charleston, Cathy Linh Che, Don Mee Choi, Franny Choi, Kyeong-Hee Choi, Bruce Cumings, Gregory Djanikian, Tarfia Faizullah, Amanda Galvan Huynh, Andre Haag, Kimiko Hahn, Joseph Han, Richie Hofmann, Sam Ikehara, Yoojung Jang, Miguel Jiménez, Jack Jung, Crystal Hana Kim, Kim Hyesoon, E. J. Koh, Yusef Komunyakaa, Elliot Lam, Sally Wen Mao, Kenneth May, Jeffrey McDaniel, Sharon Olds, Sandra Park, Eilin Pérez, Srikanth (Chicu) Reddy, Sabine Schulz, Charles Simic, Monica Sok, Christopher Soto, Susan Su, Ocean Vuong, Sam Herschel Wein, Sungik Yang, and Javier Zamora. Thank you for everything you've taught me over the years about showing up for our writing and for one another. Kien Lam, how fortunate is it that we can turn to each other with our super rough drafts of poems and jokes so we become better at both. I can always trust you to help me see everything with more clarity and joy.

Tremendous appreciation and warmth to my dear pals, especially Carol Han and Minkwang Jang, and to my family, for their endless encouragement and trust, even though poetry may not be their main jam. I love that I can make you proud.

Sometimes I am still in disbelief that Dan Halpern is my editor and Jin Auh is my agent. It has been an absolute honor to put my work in these legends' care. My life, no doubt, became a thousand times cooler with them in it. Dan, Jin, thank you for your faith, for your reading; it has meant more to me than I can express.

Oceans of gratitude to Noah Hoff, Rob Shapiro, Bonnie Thompson, Elizabeth Schraft, Ian Gibbs, Melissa Yoon, and everyone at Alfred A. Knopf who had a hand in assuring this book into being, and to my sweet colleagues at the Asian American Writers' Workshop and the University of Hawai'i at Mānoa for supporting my critical and creative work.

David Krolikoski, our love is my favorite. As I said on our wedding day, I celebrate all the choices and forces in the universe that led to us. I stay astounded that I get to stand next to you, through all that is gorgeous and terrifying in this world and life. Thank you for holding me in ways I didn't even know I needed before I met you. Thank you for your grace, tenderness, patience, and wisdom. This book is for you.

A NOTE ABOUT THE AUTHOR

Emily Jungmin Yoon is the author of *Ordinary Misfortunes* and *A Cruelty Special to Our Species,* a finalist for the 2020 Kate Tufts Discovery Award, Claremont Graduate University, and the winner of the 2019 Devil's Kitchen Reading Award in poetry. Yoon is the recipient of awards and fellowships from the Poetry Foundation, the Bread Loaf Writers' Conference, and *Ploughshares,* and her work has appeared in *The New Yorker, Poetry, The New York Times Magazine, The Paris Review,* and *The Sewanee Review.* Yoon is the poetry editor for *The Margins,* the literary magazine of the Asian American Writers' Workshop, and she is an assistant professor of Korean literature at the University of Hawai'i at Mānoa. She splits her time between Honolulu and South Korea.

A NOTE ON THE TYPE

This book was set in Scala, a typeface designed by the Dutch designer Martin Majoor (b. 1960) in 1988 and released by the FontFont foundry in 1990. While designed as a fully modern family of fonts containing both a serif and a sans serif alphabet, Scala retains many refinements normally associated with traditional fonts.

Composed by North Market Street Graphics,
Lancaster, Pennsylvania

Printed and bound by Friesens,
Altona, Manitoba

Designed by Soonyoung Kwon